FROM CHUCK NORRIS TO THE KARATE KID
Martial Arts in the Movies

By Suzanne Weyn and Ellen Steiber

PARACHUTE
PRESS, INC.

Parachute Press, Inc.
200 Fifth Avenue, Rm 461
New York, New York 10010

First printing August 1986
Printed in the U.S.A.

Typeset by Paragraphics, Inc.

PHOTO CREDITS:

Photos on pages 29 and 30 (top)/**Globe Photos.**
Photos on pages 32, 33, 34, 37 (bottom), 39 (top)/
courtesy of **WW Entertainment.**
Photo of *Sanjuro* on page 39 used courtesy of **The
Museum of Modern Art/Film Stills Archive.**
Photo on page 40/**Tri-Star Pictures.**
Photos on pages 41, 42, 43, and 44/**Columbia Pictures.**
Cover photo of Chuck Norris/**Sygma Photo News.**

CONTENTS

The authors would like to thank the following people for their time and help:

Bill and Karen Palmer, coauthors of *Martial Arts Movies*

Sylvia Delia of WW Entertainment

Alan Paul of *American Karate* magazine

Maureen Lynch

and the teachers and students of Seido Karate

Introduction

The days when heroes clobbered their enemies with regular old punches are all but gone. Today, a neat karate chop or a quick judo flip are more the style. Tune in to your favorite TV adventure show or spend the afternoon at the movies and chances are you'll see at least one thrilling martial arts move. The fighting styles of the Orient are now the method of choice for modern American movie stars.

Two of the most famous and popular American martial arts heroes are Ralph Macchio, better known as the Karate Kid, and Chuck Norris. These two film favorites couldn't be more different from each other. Yet both of them have brought the martial arts to American movies as never before. Millions thrill to Chuck's spinning back-kicks and no-nonsense approach. Just as many root for the gentle Karate Kid as he fights to victory in the big showdown tournament.

How did these stars get started? How much of the fighting you see on the movie screen is real? How dangerous can it be? Just wait—we're about to answer all your questions!

We'll also go back and take a look at the original martial arts movies of Japan and China—films that starred the great Bruce Lee and other amazing fighters.

So sit back and enjoy this tour of the martial arts in movies. When you're done, you'll never look at a movie fight scene the same way again.

Chuck Norris: America's High-Kicking Hero

Chuck Norris, the most famous American martial artist, is now the undefeated six-time winner of the karate middleweight championship and a top movie star! But no one handed him success. He had to fight for it every step of the way.

Things weren't easy for Chuck when he was a kid. He was born in 1940 to an extremely poor family in Ryan, Oklahoma. Carlos Ray Norris, as he was then called, was the oldest of three boys. "My mother worked very hard in a laundry, but we were often hungry," he remembers. His father was a hard drinker and left the family before Chuck was twelve.

Chuck had a hard time in school as well. He says he felt like "a real bust in school. I never got up in front of the class and spoke. As for physical abilities, I had none."

When Chuck was twelve, his family moved to Torrance, California. It was tough trying to meet new friends, adjust to a new school, and baby-sit for his two brothers while his mother worked. But Chuck found a wonderful escape from his troubles at the movies. He loved Westerns starring John Wayne or Gary Cooper. "John Wayne was my substitute father growing up," Chuck remembers. "He was a man who stood on his own two feet, faced controversy, dealt with it—a man who was patriotic, a man who had moral values."

Chuck's hard luck began to change when he met Dianne Holechek, a girl who went to his high school. Says Dianne, "He was just nice, clean-cut, and looked intelligent. He thinks he was very shy, but he had an air of confidence. I wanted to find out what was happening in his head."

Chuck recalls that it took him "a month to muster the courage to talk to her." But when he did, the two hit it off. They were married in 1958, right after graduating from high school. The Norrises have been lucky (and tried hard)—they are still married today.

Soon after that, Chuck joined the Air Force and was stationed in Korea. There, he began learning karate. "I studied it because I wanted to be a police officer when I got home, and I thought it would help," Chuck explains. It sure did help—but not in the way he expected.

When Chuck got out of the Air Force in 1962, he got a job as a file clerk for a company called Northrop Aviation. In the evenings, he taught karate to make extra money. He did this for two years and never did get around to taking the police test. In 1964, Chuck started a martial arts school of his own. He was a popular teacher and he soon had so many students that he opened up two more schools.

Then he started to enter competitions, and that made him train harder than ever before. Soon, he was winning lots of tournaments and feeling really good about his abilities as a martial artist. "After a while I got such a swelled head that I felt I could beat anyone," he admits.

Once Chuck became known as an unbeatable champion, even more students poured into his schools. By the age of 32, Chuck Norris was a huge success. Many people would have felt content to stop right there. Not Chuck. He wanted a new challenge. The person who offered it to him was Bruce Lee! They met at a New York tournament. The two men admired each other's skills and soon became friends.

When Bruce became the technical adviser in the 1969 Dean Martin movie *The Wrecking Crew,* he hired Chuck to appear in the film and to be a fight coordinator. Chuck speaks only one line in the movie. Next, Bruce hired Chuck to help choreograph fights in his Chinese-produced movie *Return of the Dragon*. Chuck appears in the final fight scene filmed at the Colosseum in Rome. It is the only time he has ever died onscreen.

While working in Hong Kong with Lee, Chuck met Chinese director Lo Wei. Lo Wei gave him a small role as a bad guy in his movie *Slaughter in San Francisco*. It was the last time Chuck would ever play a villain.

By 1974, Chuck had been bitten by the acting bug. A lot of people told him he'd never make it in the movies. At 34, they said he was too old. He was too short. He should stick with martial arts and leave the acting to actors. But Chuck didn't listen. Part by movie part, he climbed to superstardom.

Obviously, Chuck Norris loves practicing martial arts and making movies. But his family is even more important to him than his career. He keeps close to them even when he's working. His brother Aaron Norris has appeared in several small roles in his movies. Aaron also works as fight coordinator in almost all of Chuck's films.

Chuck's other brother, Wieland, died fighting in Vietnam in 1969. Chuck made *Missing in Action* and *Missing in Action 2: The Beginning* as a tribute to Wieland. "Since that time I've really felt for the MIA [Missing in Action] families," he says. "I think about them a lot." So even though Wieland is dead, Chuck keeps his memory close.

Chuck is also extremely proud of his two sons, Eric who is 20, and Mike, 23. Eric was a production assistant to his uncle Aaron on *Invasion U.S.A.* and even doubled for his father occasionally in the movie. He played a soldier in *Delta Force* and is a student at El Camino College in California. Eric thinks he might like to be a movie producer someday. Mike Norris has already starred in a major film, *Arctic Heat*. He hopes to make acting his career.

Chuck's sons grew up with an impressive father and they are extremely close to him. "It's a great feeling that my boys are not afraid to show love," says Chuck. "You can't buy that."

Dianne Norris has also studied karate, like her husband and sons. But that's not her main interest. She's hard at work running Woody's Wharf, the restaurant Chuck bought her in 1983. "I'd buy her the moon," says Chuck, "because she stood by me through the hard years." When asked about her husband, Dianne says, "I just love this guy so much. He's my best friend."

It was the love of his family, as well as his own determination, that made Chuck the star he is today. Another thing that fueled his drive and ambition was the vow he made never to be as poor as he was in his childhood. Chuck now makes over two million dollars for each movie, so he doesn't have to worry about being poor again. He hopes his audience—especially kids—will be inspired by his success. "I want kids to understand where I come from and how I made it," he says. "I use myself as an example of how someone pulled himself up from zero."

Chuck thinks that his personal image as well as the characters he plays onscreen make him popular with many types of people. "I'm going against odds and overcoming them. A lot of minorities face those odds. . . . I do something they want to do." Chuck hopes his movies can help others overcome the odds too.

A man who cares about his family and about helping others succeed may not seem to fit Chuck's tough-guy image, but he thinks it makes perfect sense. "Macho to me is a person who cares about other people," he explains, "but who can face situations head on and not hide from them . . . . Being tough and fighting, that isn't macho. When a guy has to keep proving himself by physical or mental force, then he's not secure, so he can't be macho."

Chuck has never been in a street fight. "If somebody said to me, 'I don't like your face,' I'd just say, 'Well, we all have our opinions. And sometimes I don't like it either.' You can lose your temper or deal with it psychologically. Rather than lower yourself to being a jerk, you be nice to him. The next thing you know, you'll be laughing together."

The two things Chuck is willing to fight for are his family and his country. "I'm a nut about patriotism," he admits. "I've been all over the world and I've been able to compare." Is there anything Chuck doesn't like about America? Yes, drugs. "I believe to this day that if our country is ever going to go down the tubes, it's going to be because of drugs. They are the single worst thing in our country today."

Chuck likes being thought of as an American hero. "Call it square if you want," he says, "but I'm a flag-waver, so I push a lot of Americanism in my movies. Whatever it is I'm doing, people seem to like it."

CHUCK THE FIGHTER

When Chuck Norris joined the Air Force he had one specific goal. "I was going to be the toughest thing you ever saw," he says. So when he was stationed in South Korea, he began to study the Oriental martial arts. At first he trained in judo, a Japanese sport based on the older, more deadly martial art called jujitsu. Judo consists mostly of wrestling moves and ways to throw an opponent.

One day as Chuck was walking through the village of Osan he saw an entirely different method of fighting—one that would change his life. He watched a group of Korean men practicing spectacular high-flying kicks. "I was mesmerized," he remembers. The art was tang soo do, a Korean system of unarmed fighting that is similar to karate but uses more kicks.

Chuck devoted himself to tang soo do. He worked hard, practicing up to seven hours a day, six days a week. As any martial artist knows, practicing just one hour a day can be tiring. Seven is incredible—and Chuck got incredible results! Normally, it takes three to seven years to earn a black belt. In fact there is a saying in karate that it takes three years to learn how to make a fist properly, three years to learn how to stand properly, and three years to learn how to strike a target properly. That adds up to nine years of training before you can stand still and throw a punch—*properly!* Of course, this refers to the perfect master's punch. Chuck Norris was the proof that someone who trained hard—really hard—could go further than anyone dreamed. Only a year after he started studying martial arts, he returned home with a brown belt in judo and a black belt in karate!

More important, something inside him had changed. "By the time I came back," he says, "I didn't need to be tough. When you master something, when you have the ability and discipline, you don't need to prove it."

At home, Chuck earned a second black belt in tae kwon do, another Korean style similar to karate, and began teaching the fighting arts as a second job. Chuck's schools succeeded because, like all good martial arts instructors, he tried to teach more than just fighting. "We're not interested in training killers in twelve weeks," he said. "The art of karate is to train yourself in the body so as to develop the mind. The physical is only a vehicle to strengthen yourself psychologically and mentally. A lot of kids come in and say, 'I want to be tough.' That's only insecurity."

In the United States, competing in tournaments is the best way to become known as a martial artist, and there are many different kinds of tournaments. In full-contact fighting, opponents use full-power kicks and punches. Today, it's the most popular kind of competition. But when Chuck Norris began fighting in the 1960s, the protective safety gear that fighters now use hadn't been developed. Fights were won by scoring points. In the point system, the fight is stopped every time someone scores a point by striking a target area. Tournaments have very strict rules about where you can hit someone and which techniques can be used. For example, elbow strikes are common in karate and perfect for self-defense, but they're not used in competitive fighting.

Recalling those days, Chuck explains, "Until recently, none of the blows were allowed to land in a match. The idea is to develop tremendous control so that a blow or kick can come this close"—Chuck holds his thumb and forefinger an inch apart. "That's the art." It was an art that would be very useful when Chuck began to make movies.

Although he was a good teacher when he first opened his school, back then Chuck was not a great martial artist. It took an embarrassing situation to help turn him into a great competitor. He entered his first tournament with three of his students. "My three students won," he says, "and I lost!"

But Chuck didn't let himself get discouraged. He just trained harder. "I got beat at first," he admits, "but the only time you ever fail is when you don't learn from losing. There are three areas of winning—the physical, the mental, and the emotional. I trained by teaching my classes eight hours a day, and I beat a lot of guys who were better than I am because I didn't get tired. When somebody gets tired, you see it in his eyes, you see him thinking, 'I've had enough. I want to go home.'"

On the tournament circuit, Chuck became famous for his arsenal of kicks. In his most famous one, he would surprise his opponent by beginning a front kick, then pivoting so that suddenly his leg would be coming from a completely different direction.

A year after he began competing in tournaments, Chuck won the California state title. This was only the beginning. Between 1965 and 1974 Chuck Norris won every major martial arts title, including the national title, the World Professional Middleweight Championship, the International Grand Karate Championship, and the All-American Grand Championship.

In 1969 Chuck was given the Triple Crown for the highest number of tournament wins, and *Black Belt* magazine named him Fighter of the Year. But the biggest title of all came in 1970 when he won the Golden Fist award for Fighter of the Decade!

Chuck credits his spectacular record to the mental-image drills he used to do before each match. For example, he'd imagine his opponent throwing a particular kick and then see himself blocking the kick perfectly.

Chuck also had another advantage. "I'd studied all forms," he explains. "Korean karate is mostly the feet, Japanese is mostly the hands, and Chinese is mobility, so if I fought a Korean, I'd use my hands, and if I fought a Japanese, I'd use my feet." Chuck became an expert in strategy, fighting with techniques that his opponents couldn't match.

Although Chuck traveled throughout the country on the tournament circuit, he still found time to teach. Many of his black belt students went on to become tournament superstars in their own right. In fact, he has more winning students than almost any other coach in the United States. Chuck also taught his own brother, Aaron, and several celebrities, including the Osmond Brothers, the late Steve McQueen, and Priscilla Presley.

In 1970, Chuck was named to the World Professional Team. His teammates included fellow karate legends Mike Stone, Joe Lewis, Skipper Mullins, and Bob Wall. The team defeated all challengers. They were so successful that after their first big victory, no one else would fight them.

Chuck competed until 1974. After that, he became a tournament official. Ben Perry, a former fighter who appeared in four of Chuck's films, remembers, "He was a great referee. Very fair." Tournament referees not only have to be honest, they have to have what are called "good eyes"—they have to see *everything*, and in a sport based on lightning-fast moves that is rarely easy. In the 1973 Battle of Atlanta, Chuck was given an Outstanding Official award.

In 1975, Chuck was one of the co-founders of the National Karate League—twelve full-contact karate teams based in cities throughout the country.

Even though Chuck has gone from competition winner to instructor to referee to movie star, he has never given up the basis of it all—his martial arts training. Along with his sons, Mike and Eric, he still does daily three-hour workouts. These extra-rigorous practice sessions combine kicking and punching drills with free weights and cardiovascular aerobic training.

The martial arts will always remain vital to Chuck Norris. "These studies changed my entire life," he says. "For the first time I realized that there was nothing I couldn't achieve if I just had the determination and persistence. In gaining the ability to defend myself, I also learned the discipline and self-respect I need for the rest of my life."

CHUCK NORRIS'S ACTION-PACKED MOVIES

Everyone knows Chuck Norris as a movie star. Yet acting was the most difficult challenge in his life. "I was not a natural actor," he admits. "I had to learn."

He got into acting gradually, starting with small parts which his friend Bruce Lee gave to him.

It was one of his students, the late actor Steve McQueen, who suggested that Chuck take acting seriously. "He told me I should think about projecting a presence and never do a part that had a lot of dialogue," he says. "He told me, 'Movies are visual and when you try to verbalize something, you're going to lose the audience.'"

Chuck took Steve McQueen's advice and looked for roles that were low on talking and high in action. But he also knew that becoming a successful actor would mean a lot of hard work. So he went ahead and did a very risky but courageous thing. He sold his three karate schools and used the money from the sales to live on while he studied full time with the famous acting coach Lee Strasberg. He spent as many as thirty hours a week in acting classes. "It was difficult at times," he remembers. "The basis of karate is to control your emotions. For acting, I had to exploit my emotions for all they were worth."

Graduating from the Lee Strasberg Institute for actors was only the first step. The next one was trying to get cast in a movie. In 1977, he got the starring role in *Breaker, Breaker.* In that film, he did a lot of kicking and very little talking. He played a trucker who faces all kinds of bad guys. It wasn't a great movie, but it was the first time Chuck starred in a movie as the good guy.

But Chuck just wasn't happy with the roles he was being offered, so he decided to create his own movie projects. He asked one of his former karate students to write a script—and that was the beginning of *Good Guys Wear Black.* It's the story of a Vietnam vet who saves the men of his old unit from a killer who's out to get them.

Chuck brought the script to Hollywood, but no one was interested. Not willing to accept defeat, he and a young producer made the movie themselves. In less than a year, it was a hit that had earned eighteen million dollars!

Though the movie made a lot of money, the critics didn't think Chuck was much of an actor. Even Chuck himself wasn't too happy with it. "The first time I saw the film, I thought it wasn't bad," he says. "By the fourth time, however, I was hiding in embarrassment."

Chuck took the money from *Good Guys Wear Black* and helped to finance his next project, *A Force of One*. This time, even *The New York Times* admitted that the movie was pretty good. In *A Force of One*, Chuck played a cop who single-handedly smashes a drug ring. In fact, to make his point, Chuck karate-chops a box full of drugs in midair. Chuck's next movie was *The Octagon*, made in 1981. It was even more successful than his other films. Chuck plays a karate champ who eventually must fight an entire Ninja training camp all alone.

Although Chuck's movies were hits at the box office, it still bothered him that critics didn't usually like them. "The sensitive side of me hated being blasted every time," he admits. "They'd say: 'Why doesn't Chuck get back to karate school where he belongs.' That hurt. Look, I never attempted to be a Dustin Hoffman. I'm just trying to create an image on the screen that I hope people will enjoy seeing."

Despite the criticism, Chuck went on to make *An Eye for an Eye*, *Forced Vengeance*, and *Silent Rage*. In 1983, he made *Lone Wolf McQuade* with TV's

Kung Fu star David Carradine. He thinks it was the turning point in his career. At last, the general public, not just martial arts fans, came to see one of his movies. In it, Chuck played a Texas Ranger who bends the law to make sure justice is served.

After that, Chuck made *Missing in Action* and its sequel, *Missing in Action 2: The Beginning*. Then came *Code of Silence, Invasion U.S.A.*, and *Delta Force.* Each movie was a hit.

Chuck believes that a lot of his popularity comes from old-fashioned values of the characters he plays. "The endings are always positive," he says of his movies. "I think a lot of people are tired of depressing, boring films. I think they like to feel good at the end of a film. One of the biggest thrills of my life came when I went to a theater to see *Missing in Action* and all the people stood up and applauded at the end.

Chuck knows some people think his movies are too violent. "I'm not provoking violence," he says. "What I'm trying to project is how to deal with it. But to deal with violence, you've got to show violence."

It's important to Chuck that his movie characters share his own values. That's why he co-wrote *Invasion U.S.A.* and makes sure he has final approval on all his scripts. "When I'm in a movie, I can have whatever name I want for a character, but in the minds of the kids who come to see the film, it's still Chuck Norris."

Chuck doesn't mind that his character is always the same. "You've got to know where your limitations are," he observes. "My abilities are not that high, although I think I've definitely improved as an actor. I really enjoy positive action-type films. I like seeing them and I like doing them."

What's in the future for Chuck Norris? A lot more movies, that's for sure. He's negotiated a multi-million dollar deal with a movie company to produce his next fourteen movies. But now he's trying to play down his martial arts reputation. He won't be photographed in karate poses anymore. He wants to branch out into movies that have more complex plots and a bit less fighting.

Chuck Norris fans need not fear, though. No matter what kind of movie he does in the future, you can bet it will be full of his special spine-tingling excitement.

10 FACTS ABOUT CHUCK NORRIS

1. His license plate reads TOPKICK.

2. He is part English, part Irish, and part Cherokee Indian.

3. He is 5'10" and weighs 170 pounds.

4. He doesn't smoke.

5. He grew his beard to cover the sixteen stitches he received near his mouth while filming *Missing in Action*.

6. He has framed paintings of his heroes Clark Gable, Gary Cooper, and John Wayne hanging in his home office.

7. He is 46 years old.

8. He has a weakness for vanilla ice cream with walnuts.

9. He has fractured his nose four times, his shoulder twice, and his toes often.

10. He is the only martial artist to have been named three times to the Black Belt Hall of Fame. He was "Fighter of the Year" (1969), "Instructor of the Year" (1975), and "Man of the Year" (1977).

Back to the Beginning: Hong Kong Chopsockies

Although martial arts movies have been coming out of Hong Kong for over sixty years, most of the early ones, like *The Burning of the Red Lotus Temple* (1929) and *Bloody Fights* (1933), were pretty tame. The actors were usually not skilled martial artists and their moves were choreographed more like dances than fight scenes. When a hero pulled off some unbelievable leap or jump, it was usually with the help of wire contraptions and pulleys.

The first really active martial arts movies came out in 1949. They were part of a series about a real-life character named Huang Fei-Hong. He lived from 1847 to 1924. This kung fu expert was skilled in medicine and as a lion dancer. Lion dancing is an ancient art that uses the moves of martial arts techniques. One dancer makes the heavy puppet-like head of the lion costume come alive while another dances beneath the costume's tail. Lion dancing calls for great physical skill.

What made movies about Huang Fei-Hong different was that their star, Kwan Tak Hing, was really a lion dancer and an amazing martial artist. Kwan Tak Hing insisted on realism in his movies and enacted all the fight scenes himself.

Most of the old movies were about characters who fought because of pride and greed. Not Huang Fei-Hong. He was a healer and a man of peace who practiced kung fu as an art and fought only in self-defense. He was a gentle hero, like the ones later played by David Carradine and Ralph Macchio.

Then came Bruce Lee! More than any other single person, Bruce is responsible for making martial arts movies popular in Western countries. He had the fighting skills, the charisma, and the talent as an actor to do it!

Bruce appeared on American television in the late 1960s and early 70s. His success here, as well as his reputation as a child star in Hong Kong, earned him starring roles in three Hong Kong-made movies: *The Big Boss*, *Fist of Fury*, and *Way of the Dragon*. These movies were great successes in China. As a result, a Hollywood producer named Fred Weintraub offered to star him in a big-budget American movie called *Enter the Dragon*.

Many feel *Enter the Dragon* is one of the greatest martial arts movies ever made. It caused a wave of demand for other martial arts films in America and it set the style for all martial arts movies made after it. After *Enter the Dragon* was released in 1973, audiences wanted to see more of Bruce Lee —much more. To meet this demand, Bruce's Hong Kong films were brought over and given new names. *The Big Boss* was named *Fists of Fury. Fist of Fury* became *The Chinese Connection*, and *Way of the Dragon* was advertised as a sequel to *Enter the Dragon* even though it had been made first. It was renamed *Return of the Dragon.*

Sadly, Bruce Lee died on July 20, 1973, just as he was about to become the most successful Chinese star in the world! A flood of movies done by Bruce Lee imitators were made in a hurry to cash in on Bruce's popularity. They were generally pretty awful. Rip-off movies like *Bruce Lee Super-dragon* (1974), *Exit the Dragon, Enter the Tiger* (1976), *Fist of Fury II* (1976), *Bruce Lee the Invincible* (1977), and *Bruce Lee's Secret* (1977) featured inferior martial artists who called themselves names like Bruce Li, Bruce Le, Dragon Lee, and Bronson Lee.

The only real Bruce Lee movie that came out after his death was called *Game of Death.* Bruce had started filming the movie just before he died. It featured Bruce's friend and student, the basketball star Kareem Abdul-Jabbar. The producers spliced together some of the already-filmed scenes and hired doubles to do the rest. The resulting movie is pretty much a mess, but it is the last film in which Bruce Lee really appears.

Bruce Lee's popularity encouraged Hong Kong

movie companies like Golden Harvest and The Shaw Brothers to release many of their movies in the United States. These films were dubbed "chopsockies" by the American press because there was usually a lot of action but not much plot. All the same, many wonderful, exciting movies came out of Hong Kong, as well.

It's interesting to note that most of these movies are set in China's past. One reason is Chinese costumes, weapons, and philosophies make colorful, fascinating settings. Another is that China's history is full of great stories that are perfect for movie scripts. The Shaw Brothers movie *The Bloody Avengers*, for example, tells the true story of the Boxer Rebellion of 1900, in which kung fu boxers tried to get all foreigners to leave China. Invincible as these Chinese patriots felt they were, they were no match for American and British gun powder.

That brings us to another important reason why these movies are set in the past—guns. Martial artists don't really stand much chance against guns, no matter how fantastic their fighting skills are. Once you bring a martial arts movie into modern times, the writer has to figure out how the hero avoids getting shot by the bad guys. It can be done, but it's easier (and fairer) just to set the movie in a period when guns simply weren't around.

Besides Bruce Lee, there were other talented

Chinese martial arts actors. Ti Lung and his sidekick David Chiang made a number of popular films in the early 1970s. Ti Lung was tall and handsome, Chiang was short, comical, and acrobatic. Two of their best movies are *Dynasty of Blood* and *Deadly Duo*. *Deadly Duo* is set in the time of the Yuan Dynasty and has the two heroes battling the Mongols. It is full of great fight scenes and it features such interesting ancient weapons as Ti Lung's battle-ax and Chiang's steel whip.

Five Masters of Death in 1975 coupled Ti Lung and David Chiang with two new stars of the martial arts cinema, Chi Kuan Chun, and the lively, acrobatic Alexander Fu Sheng. Alexander Fu Sheng was a new blend of actor/kung fu expert. He was trained in Hong Kong both to read lines well and also to be a convincing fighter. He was a graduate of the Shaw acting school.

Five Masters of Death is important because it was the first extremely successful movie to feature the legendary Shaolin Temple. This temple is the ancient birthplace of kung fu. It is where Buddhist monks first watched animals as they fought and adapted the techniques to human fighting. Now, many other films are set at the ancient Shaolin Temple.

One of the most notable of the Shaolin movies is called *Executioners of Death* (1977). It tells of the destruction of the Shaolin Temple during the Manchu Dynasty. In the movie, Hung Wen Ting (played by Yung Wang Yu) studies to avenge the destruction of the temple, and in the process he develops the hung gar fighting style. Hung gar is the style of kung fu most common to southern China and it's the one usually used in martial arts movies.

The director, Lui Chia Liang, followed *Executioners of Death* with another big hit, *Thirty-Sixth Chamber of Shaolin*. This movie, full of awe-inspiring training scenes, was called *The Master Killer* when it came to the United States. It made its lead, Liu Chia Hui, a star. He is now one of the Orient's most famous martial arts actors.

One of Liu Chia Hui's best movies was called *Legendary Weapons of Kung Fu* (1982). It told the story of how Chinese martial artists coped with Westerners who brought a new threat—guns—into their land. The movie has everything: weapons, Alexander Fu Sheng's amazing stunts (it was his comeback film after a serious injury), magical Ninjas, and a thrilling story.

The next superstar to come out of Hong Kong was Jackie Chan. He is the only actor/martial artist as popular as Liu Chia Hui today. Jackie Chan was born in 1954. He studied in a Peking opera school called the China Dramatic Academy, learning gymnastics, acrobatics, martial arts, and drama.

As an adult, he changed his name to Cheng Lung and appeared in more than ten movies before his role in *Eagle's Shadow* (1978) made him a star. Jackie Chan—that's his American name—has a light-hearted style that has won him the reputation as the "Chinese Burt Reynolds." He usually plays a bumbler who often loses his first fight with each new opponent but comes out victorious in the end.

Jackie Chan followed *Eagle's Shadow* with another success, *Drunken Master* (1979). The title refers to the kung fu technique called "drunken style." In it, experts flail their arms and appear to be off balance, as if they had indeed had too much to drink. But in truth, they are in total control—and can beat many skilled opponents with their effective fighting.

Jackie Chan wrote and directed his next film, *Fearless Hyena*. He followed that with *The Young Master* in 1980. Afterwards, he went to Hollywood where he appeared in a movie produced by Fred Weintraub called *The Big Brawl*. Jackie sewed up his image as the "new Bruce Lee" when he made *Cannonball Run* with Burt Reynolds in 1981 and the sequel in 1984. At last, the mainstream movie audience had a chance to see him perform.

Between the *Cannonball* movies, Jackie made two more terrific Chinese martial arts movies: *Dragon Lord* and *Project A*.

Project A was the name of a plan the Chinese Coast Guard developed in 1903 to rid the harbors of pirates. Jackie directed the movie and starred in it. One of the entertaining things about *Project A* is the end credits. The credit lines roll over scenes of flubbed stunts from the movie. Chan isn't afraid to laugh at himself. He shows a blooper of himself jumping off an awning and falling onto the ground by mistake.

Chinese martial arts films have come a long way since the early Huang Fei-Hong films. But the character of Huang Fei-Hong and the star who made him come alive on the movie screen, Kwan Tak Hing, are still very much a part of today's martial arts film world. Kwan Tak Hing appeared in *The Magnificent Butcher* (1980), once again playing the part of Huang Fei-Hong! In the movie's opening fight scene, the 74-year-old actor displays amazing flips, somersaults, twists, and blocks. In 1981, he helped make a modern Huang Fei-Hong movie called *Dreadnaught*, which features a lion dance as one of its highlights.

Kwan Tak Hing helped make martial arts movies the realistic and exciting films they are today. No longer the old chopsockies of years ago, fight movies now have plots, humor, and feeling—and spectacular displays of martial arts that have earned them fans all around the world.

In *Missing in Action II* Chuck played an American sergeant fighting in Vietnam.

Chuck was detective Eddie Cusack in *Code of Silence.*

As Scott James, Chuck fought mercenary terrorists who held the secret of *The Octagon.*

The famous Chuck Norris kick is demonstrated in *An Eye For an Eye*.

Popular star David Chiang (in white) showed his skill in
A Slice of Death.

Exciting fight scenes like this one from *Two Champions
of Death* are a staple of Hong Kong movies.

The acrobatic Lu Feng shows the spectacular jump that helped make him a star.

Liu Chia Hui (left) is one of the biggest martial arts stars in China.

Liu Chia Hui appears once again as the Master Killer, the role which made him a star, in *Return of the Master Killer*.

The action never stops in *A Slice of Death*.

Bruce Lee was the greatest international Chinese star.

Bruce didn't kid around when he was fighting bad guys like these in *Fists of Fury.*

No villain was a match for Bruce!

A flare for drama as well as skill as a martial artist helped make Bruce Lee great.

In Hong Kong actors study both drama and martial arts to be convincing in these exciting fight scenes.

Super Ninjas made powerful foes for these Chinese martial arts stars.

The big fight scene in *Instructors of Death*.

Super Ninjas is a Chinese-made movie which featured evil Japanese Ninjas.

Sanjuro was one of the first samurai movies.

Black belt Taimak starred in the martial arts musical *The Last Dragon*.

In *The Karate Kid*, Daniel (Ralph Macchio) studied karate from the wise Mr. Miyagi (Noriyuki "Pat" Morita).

Ralph Macchio trained hard to look and move like a real martial artist.

Elisabeth Shue played Daniel's girlfriend.

In *The Karate Kid,* Mr. Miyagi started Daniel's training with a slow program of work which actually builds strength and coordination.

In *The Karate Kid II,* Daniel is comforted by his new love, Kumiko, played by Tamlyn Tomita.

Daniel's martial arts skills grow as Mr. Miyagi prepares him for their next challenge.

The bond between Mr. Miyagi and Daniel is strengthened in *The Karate Kid II* when they meet a life and death threat together.

Bruce Lee: The Life of a Legend

Bruce Lee died just as his movies were becoming worldwide sensations. He set the stage for the many martial arts movies that were to follow his; but he was not alive to enjoy the enormous new popularity of fight films. But Bruce is still considered to be the master. To this day, no one has surpassed him in charm, believability, and sheer martial artistry.

Bruce Lee was born in San Francisco on November 27, 1940. His Oriental name was Lee Jun Fan. (In the Orient, the family name comes first.) It was the supervising doctor who dubbed young Jun Fan "Bruce." So, for the American records he was named Bruce Lee.

Bruce was born into a theatrical family. His father, Lee Hoi Chuen, was a well-known actor in both China and the United States. When Bruce was only three months old he made his acting debut in a production of a play called *Golden Gate*

Girl. As you may have guessed, Bruce played the baby.

Bruce's family returned to China when he was still small. He started appearing in Hong Kong movies at the age of six. By the age of seven he was the star of a movie called *My Son A-Chang*. Bruce was a popular child actor and he was known as "Little Dragon," since his stage name, Siu Lung, meant exactly that.

Unfortunately, young Bruce had always been a difficult child. Family and friends recall that he could never be still—he even had a tendency to sleepwalk at night! He was nervous, often sick, and suffered from nightmares. He admitted that as he grew older, he "went looking for fights."

By the time Bruce was a teenager he was often in trouble. He was already studying wing chun, a form of kung fu some consider to be quite brutal. He had the chance to use it in the many street fights he got into.

There was another side to the young man, though. He was an expert at the cha-cha, often winning contests and dancing until dawn. He was also an avid reader. He got glasses in his teens because his eyes were strained from pouring through books. Bruce Lee was clearly a young man with a lot of energy that he wasn't sure how to direct constructively.

After Bruce's great success in the movie *The Orphan*, The Shaw Brothers Studio offered him a contract. His mother said no. Bruce's personal life was so out of control and his manner so abrasive and arrogant that his mother thought the life of a movie star would destroy him. Instead, his family sent him to the United States to get an education and to grow up.

At 18, Bruce enrolled in the University of Washington. There he studied hard and taught kung fu to earn money. (He had tried working in a restaurant, but didn't like it at all.) When he was still a child, Bruce had learned the art of tai chi chuan from his father. This is a series of graceful moves that are sometimes done in order to meditate or just to exercise. But if you practice hard enough, tai chi chuan can become an amazing martial art. By mixing his knowledge of the powerful wing chun style to the gentle form of tai chi, Bruce became quite a martial artist. While he was at college, he worked on his martial arts skills and thought about them. By the age of 24, he wrote a book called *Chinese Gung-Fu: The Philosophical Art of Self Defense.* (Gung-fu is just another way of spelling kung fu.)

That same year, Bruce married Linda Emery and moved with her to California. There he became involved with the Ed Parker International Karate Championships. Martial artist Mike Stone remembers Bruce: "He did a demonstration there and I won the grand championship in the heavyweight division. Afterwards we went out for a

Chinese dinner. We became friends and would work out together one day a week. I would work out with him one day, Chuck Norris would work out with him another and so would Joe Lewis."

Film clips of Bruce performing at these demonstrations brought him to the attention of a TV producer. The man was looking for an actor to play Kato on a series called *The Green Hornet*. In 1966, Bruce got the part. The series was a flop, but everyone agreed that Bruce was the best thing in it.

All this time, Bruce kept perfecting his martial arts skills. He developed a style all his own that came to be known as jeet kune do—"the way of the intercepting fist." Part of the philosophy was that students should try hard to improve all the time and find joy in their own improvement. The style is also highly visual and makes for exciting onscreen fighting. This new style of kung fu attracted many followers, including actors, writers, and producers. Bruce's students kept hiring him for guest roles on their shows.

By now the arrogant young teen had disappeared and a serious professional with goals and ambitions had replaced him. Bruce had three jeet kune do schools and his reputation was growing, thanks to word of mouth and his appearances on TV.

In 1969, he played a terrifying bad guy in the movie *Marlowe* with James Garner. That same year, he was technical adviser for *The Wrecking Crew.* In 1971, Bruce was featured in a two-part episode of the TV series *Longstreet.* The episode was written especially for him by one of his students and it was called "The Way of the Fist." In the series, Bruce spoke of the inner peace necessary to master martial arts.

A stroke of luck opened the way for the next phase of Bruce's career. *The Green Hornet* TV series premiered in China three years after it was first shown in the United States. While Americans had given the show a cool reception, the Chinese loved it. Bruce took a promotional trip to China. He was spotted by Raymond Chow, head of Golden Harvest movies, after he appeared on a talk show. Chow signed him up for a movie contract almost immediately.

Bruce played his first starring role as a martial arts hero in *The Big Boss* (known to Americans as *Fists of Fury*). His next movie, *Fist of Fury* (known in America as *The Chinese Connection*) was made quickly to cash in on his popularity, but it was even better than the first film. In the thrilling final scene, Bruce fights off the bad guys with nunchakas, the deadly ancient weapon he was so skilled at using. Though the nunchakas are really made of hard wood, in his movie Bruce used soft clubs so that he could hit his screen opponent without knocking him senseless. The Chinese audiences went wild over *Fist of Fury.* They liked Bruce's brash style of acting and they loved his strong, direct martial arts skills.

Bruce now had the clout to form his own production company, Concord Productions. He wrote, directed, and starred in his next movie, *Way of the Dragon* (known in the U.S. as *Return of the Dragon*). In this movie, Bruce dealt with the problem of guns by having his character throw wooden darts into his enemies' gun hands. This is the movie that featured Bruce in a final fight with his real-life friend Chuck Norris.

From there Bruce came back to the United States and made *Enter the Dragon,* the movie that really kicked off American interest in martial arts movies. He supervised all the fight scenes and he also suggested the Shaolin Temple sequences that introduced Americans to the legend behind kung fu.

Bruce had enjoyed a string of successes. His big disappointment came when he was turned down for the part of Caine in the TV series *Kung Fu.* The idea was developed as a result of the movie *Enter the Dragon.* It was originally conceived as a movie idea, but Warner Television picked it up as a series. Fred Weintraub remembers, "We designed the series for Bruce."

Unfortunately, the network wasn't convinced that American audiences were ready for an Oriental leading man—even though the success of *Enter the Dragon* had proved otherwise. They hired actor David Carradine instead. "When he didn't get the part, I was stunned," Fred Weintraub recalls. "Bruce was heartbroken."

Disappointing as that was, Bruce had a lot to be happy about. He was discussing his second American project (for which he would be paid a million dollars, a top salary at that time), he was on the verge of signing a contract with the Chinese movie studio, The Shaw Brothers. And he was beginning an independent movie of his own to be called *Game of Death*.

Bruce Lee died suddenly at the age of 33. He had a type of blood clot called an aneurism in his brain. Some say this was the result of a fall he took on the set of *Game of Death*. Some have implied that drug abuse caused the clot. Producer Fred Weintraub doesn't believe that Bruce used drugs. He says, "Bruce would never put anything into his body that would hurt him. I had him examined at UCLA the week before he died. He was in great shape."

Bruce lived a short life, but it was full of great inner growth and worldly successes. Through his movies, the marvelous Bruce Lee lives on. He will never be forgotten.

15 FACTS ABOUT BRUCE LEE

1. He was injured during the filming of *Enter the Dragon* because he insisted on using an undefanged snake (he was bitten) and a real bottle instead of a movie-fake breakaway bottle (he was cut with it).

2. He practiced his quick draw with a piece of quick-draw equipment once owned by Sammy Davis Jr.

3. He had two older sisters and a younger brother.

4. Wing chun, the martial art he first studied, is the only form of kung fu created by a woman.

5. He once played a martial arts teacher on an episode of *Ironside,* starring Raymond Burr.

6. The first time audiences heard his famous animal screeches was in the movie *Fists of Fury.* He used them only in movies, not in real workouts.

7. He was so nervous on the first day of filming *Enter the Dragon* that he had to do one scene over 27 times.

8. Before he became a big movie star, he was the highest-paid martial arts teacher in America.

9. He won the Crown Colony Cha-Cha Dancing Championship in 1958.

10. He also won the Inter-School Boxing Championship in Hong Kong shortly after taking up martial arts. It is the only martial arts title he ever won (or tried for).

11. He held no rank in martial arts, nor did he want one. He once said: "Unless you can really do it, that belt doesn't mean anything. I think it might be useful to hold your pants up." Mr. Miyagi in *The Karate Kid* was echoing Bruce's sentiments when he told Daniel that his only belt was the canvas one on his pants.

12. He wrote and illustrated his *Tao of Jeet Kune Do.* His wife had it published by Ohara Publications in 1975.

13. He had trouble keeping weight on. To stay healthy he drank a special mixture several times a day. It was made out of Real Blair protein powder, vegetable oil, peanut flour, powdered milk dissolved in ice water, eggs and their shells, and sometimes bananas. He also drank a blend of freshly squeezed carrots, apples, and celery.

14. He loved cars. When he lived in California he owned a Porsche. In Hong Kong he bought himself a Mercedes 350 SL. Just before he died, he ordered a gold Rolls Royce Corniche.

15. He is buried at Lake View Cemetery just outside of Seattle, Washington.

What's Real and What's Fake in the Martial Arts Movies?

One unarmed man stands surrounded by five others, each carrying a weapon. Sword, spear, chain, knife, and nunchukas close in. Suddenly, the hero flips into the air, somersaults over his attackers' heads, and lands neatly outside their circle. Then instead of doing the sensible thing—running—he launches into a series of dazzling flying kicks. Moments later, all five attackers lie on the ground, stunned. Our hero walks calmly away with barely a scratch.

Martial arts movies are fun, but sometimes you have to wonder just how realistic they are. What is it we're seeing when we watch these incredible fights? Are all those blows really landing? How many of the scenes rely on stuntmen or special effects?

There are at least three answers for each of these questions. That's because different directors have very different ways of approaching the martial arts. Perhaps the best way to understand this is to go behind the scenes and listen to the martial artists who've worked on both American and Hong Kong films.

Chuck Norris does all his own fighting, and he doesn't use stuntmen. The actors you see fighting in his films are all real martial artists who train specially with Chuck for their parts. Ben Perry was one of those fighter/actors. He had been a tournament fighter who met Chuck at the Battle of Atlanta. They became friends and Ben became Chuck's training partner, working out at the Norris home five days a week. Soon, Perry found himself invited to fight on film. He appeared in four of Chuck's earlier movies.

To give you an idea of what training with Chuck Norris was like, imagine this schedule: Arrive at Chuck's house at seven in the morning and go for a five-mile run. Return to the house for three-minute drills. First punch the heavy bag for three minutes (this alone can make your arms feel like lead). Then do three minutes each of sit-ups, shadow-boxing, push-ups, and stretching. Now you're ready for warm-up kicks, and then slow isometric kicks, making sure that the muscles really extend and tighten. Even for someone in top shape these drills make a grueling workout.

"Training for films," Perry explains, "was the same as morning workouts except more intense." The workouts were followed by rehearsals of the actual fight scenes in the movie, and the fighters tried to react as naturally as possible to the punches and kicks their film opponents threw. Chuck's fights are shorter than those in the Chinese films and the techniques are not as flowery. They're closer to real self-defense situations. His fight scenes are some of the more realistic ones ever filmed.

Although all of Chuck's fighters were in top condition and the scenes were done with great control, there were unavoidable risks. Ben Perry will always remember one specific kick in *Octagon*. "It was a tough scene for Chuck to do," he says, "because his back was to me completely. He had to listen until I got close enough and then deliver the kick." The kick cracked Perry's sternum and broke a rib. Worse, the same scene had to be reshot six more times. "The second time," Perry says, "I came running out and stopped because I knew he was going to nail me in the same place. And he did." In that same movie, Chuck also broke another actor's rib. Though this sounds pretty brutal, keep in mind that injuries are quite common in the martial arts—especially among those who've been fighting for years. Everyone works hard to be as careful as possible—and everyone knows that an occasional accident is part of the game.

One way to avoid injuries on the set is the use of breakaway props. If you see a table shatter when a fighter lands on it, you can bet that it's specially built to crack on impact. Breakaway props are especially common in the classic scenes where a master punches through boards. But remember, an actor might use breakaway boards in the movies but still be capable of shattering a regular board in real life. Almost all the martial artists you see on film have done real breaking as part of their training. Boards, bricks, blocks of ice, even granite rocks can be destroyed using the bare hand—and tremendous concentration. But on film, it's a lot quicker, cheaper, and safer to use a convincing prop.

Another stunt secret is the air bag. When you see people jump from the roof of a building and land safely on their feet, you're watching the magic of film editing. In reality, the actors are falling onto a gigantic air bag that cushions their fall. Then another scene is shot with them on the ground, perhaps crouching as if coming out of the jump. Later in the cutting room, the film editor splices the two scenes together so that the scene of the actors jumping from the roof is followed by the one where they're on the ground. The actual air bag landing is cut out.

In most American films, the blows are faked so that they do not actually connect. Years ago in films, especially Westerns, fight scenes were for real. Actors slugged it out on cue, and black eyes and broken jaws were not uncommon. Then John

Wayne and Yakima Canutt devised the "pass blow punch." Dan Inosanto, one of Bruce Lee's most famous students (and the man who taught Bruce how to use the nunchukas), has acted and fought in many martial arts films. In his book *Absorb What Is Useful* he explains how the pass blow punch works: It "doesn't connect with the body but appears to. The fist comes as close as one foot away from contact. At that instant the fist should hit, the person receiving the blow snaps his head back. It looks as if he's received a punch when he did not. The camera sees the punch going in and records the head snapping back. Most movie fights are done this way."

The Hong Kong movies have a different approach. Cynthia Rothrock found that out when she made a film called *Yes, Madam*. Rothrock has been a top tournament fighter and this country's forms champion for five years running. Although she says she didn't have to train as much on the set as she did for tournaments, working in the movies was much harder than she'd expected. And what was hardest was the reality of the fighting. "I thought that when you go over there, it would be fake," she says. "It's actually like real street fighting. They really come at you hard. And you really have to block hard. . . . It's the first time I ever had to use my full power, whether attacking or defending. . . . I got hit in the nose with a sword, fighting against four people with swords.

I got hit before I turned. I thought, 'Well, they'll watch me. They won't hit me.' But you really have to watch out for yourself."

Of course, even in Hong Kong control is used on the set. No director wants injured actors, and no actor has the energy to hit or kick with full strength take after take. Remember, many scenes are shot over and over. No one would survive the making of a movie if all the techniques were real and done at full power.

But whether or not the blows land, you can't help but notice what incredible athletes the kung fu actors are. Though kung fu doesn't give out black belts, many of the stars have the skills of a fifth-degree black belt combined with those of a world-class gymnast. No, they don't really leap several stories at a single bound, but they do perform most of the techniques you see. Being able to do a jump kick over another actor's head is not unusual.

As for actually getting hit, well, these martial artists are protected by their own "hard bodies." Most of them have trained since the age of five, so not only are they exceptionally powerful, but their bodies have been hardened specifically for fighting. For example, getting hit on the shin is normally a very painful experience—but not for these actors. They've done so much target work kicking with their shins that they no longer have much sensation there. A thick layer of scar tissue has numbed them. They don't even feel a blow that would make a normal person limp.

With all these actors capable of legitimate, flashy fighting, why do the Hong Kong directors even bother with corny special effects? After all, it's more exciting to watch a hero really leap over a villain's head than to fly on the end of a wire to a rooftop. But believe it or not, there's a good reason for many of these weird effects.

American martial arts movies are usually action stories with a hero or villain who just happens to be a dynamic fighter. But in Chinese kung fu movies the plots center much more on the martial art itself. There are so many scenes of people training and fighting that if you took the martial arts out of the movies, you wouldn't have much more than the credits left.

Almost all of the plot lines in Chinese kung fu movies are based on Chinese history and legends. These legends tell ancient stories about men and women who devoted their entire lives to the fighting arts. Naturally, they developed powers way beyond those of ordinary humans. Just how much power, no one really knows, but the legends claim that some of these masters could jump straight up into trees. So when you see something like that in a movie, the film is actually being faithful to the legends of the martial arts. Even some of the stranger weapons, like the iron fan, were really part of Chinese history.

Any martial artist will tell you that no one fights the way they do in the movies. Real fights are shorter and uglier. Even martial arts masters wouldn't bother with the beautiful, flowery techniques you see on film if they were confronted with a real attacker. William Oliver is a fifth-degree black belt, known throughout the tournament world for his powerful fighting and fine, classical karate form. Kicking a much larger opponent in the head is no problem for him, but asked if he would do that in a street fight, he answered, "Why take the time to get your leg all the way up there? It's easier and quicker to use your hands or kick low."

When movie fights are planned out ahead of time, the fight choreographer must find a middle ground between what is practical and what is theatrical. When Bruce Lee was in *The Green Hornet*, he found that wing chun movements were too quick and not spectacular enough on film. So he added things like high combination kicks to make the fights look exciting. "You could say he designed two distinct systems," writes Dan Inosanto, "jeet kune do and the theatrical martial arts."

The most important thing about a movie fight is that it make the audience believe that the actors are really doing martial arts. It must entertain the people watching. It doesn't have to be—and rarely is—accurate as a fight.

But the best martial films go one step further.

Bill Palmer, one of the authors of a terrific book called *Martial Arts Movies*, explains that in a first-rate fight scene, the audience is "set up." You watch two actors, fighting, hoping all the time that the good guy is going to connect with a good kick. But he doesn't. Every time he throws a punch, the bad guy blocks it. The camera moves back and forth, following the rhythm of the fight. Then suddenly, the good guy does something completely unexpected and usually very simple. At just the right moment, he sweeps the villain off his feet. And you wind up as surprised as the bad guy.

In fact, what the director has done by drawing you in this way is to get you *inside* the fight. And this insider's view may be the most realistic thing of all in the martial arts movies. In the best of them, you get to experience the rhythm and strategy of a fight, and then, just like the hero, walk away with barely a scratch.

The Last Dragon:
A Martial Arts Musical

Imagine a spectacular martial arts movie with big music stars like Stevie Wonder and Smokey Robinson singing the songs and you have *The Last Dragon*.

The story is about a black teenager, Leroy Green, who is devoted to the legend of his hero, Bruce Lee. In the end, when he beats two of the nastiest guys in screen history, he assumes the power-giving name of Bruce Lee-Roy.

Taimak, who plays Leroy Green, won the role because of his acting skills and his good looks, but also because he is a karate student and instructor. He holds a third-degree black belt and is working hard toward a fourth degree. He is also a kick-boxing champion. In high school, he was a member of the fencing team and of the wrestling team. Just like Leroy, he first became interested in martial arts at the age of four when he saw Bruce Lee play Kato on *The Green Hornet*.

There is another black belt featured in the movie, a kid named Ernie Reys Jr. He is so good at karate that he has adult classification as a fighter! He is one of only a small handful of children in this country who hold black belts. Even as a toddler, he was learning from his father, Ernie Reys Sr., a well-known martial arts champion and competitor. Starting young is how he got where he is today. Look for Ernie Reys Jr. to be an important martial arts movie star in the future.

There's no other movie like *The Last Dragon*. It combines the fun of music videos, the suspense of a good story, and realistic martial arts to make one incredible film.

Japanese Films:
The Return of the Ninja

The Samurai and the Ninja are fighting characters right out of Japanese history. The Samurai warrior lived by *bushido*, the way of the sword. The Samurai were members of noble Samurai families—families who often warred with one another. By the tenth century, the only way to become a Samurai was to be born into a Samurai family. By the 1500s the Samurai families ruled Japan.

Then there were the Ninjas. They didn't belong to noble families, and they didn't follow *bushido*, or any other rules. They were deadly assassins who hired themselves out to do any dirty work they were paid for. The only philosophy they followed was to do whatever was required in order to finish a job successfully. They swore to kill themselves if they were caught. Because they did not follow *bushido*, it was believed that Ninjas had no place in the afterlife. They were true outlaws. Ninjas, although they are Japanese bad guys, have always fascinated Americans. Maybe because they existed for a relatively short period in history, you don't see many of them in Japanese movies.

You can often see Japanese Ninjas in Chinese kung fu movies because many of those stories, especially films made in the 1960s, are about problems between the Chinese and the Japanese. In the Chinese films, of course, the Japanese characters were usually the bad guys—and there was no "badder" Japanese bad guy than the Ninja!

Japanese martial arts films are different from Chinese movies in several ways. First, there is the Samurai sword. It is generally considered to have been the finest in the world, so it often plays a big role in Japanese martial arts movies.

Another difference in Japanese movies, especially earlier ones, is that the stories are generally more interesting and complicated. The high quality of these movies is often attributed to the genius of a film director named Akira Kurosawa. In 1945, Kurosawa wrote and directed *Judo Saga*, about his life. This and his other films *The Most Beautiful* and *The Men Who Tread on the Tiger's Tail* are martial arts movies at their most serious. They were banned in this country during World War II.

After World War II, Kurosawa continued to make fine movies like *Seven Samurai* (1952) and *Yojimbo* (The Bodyguard; 1961), but a new kind of

Samurai movie was also springing up. It was more bloody than ever before.

One popular Japanese hero is Zatoichi, a blind master swordsman! He is based on a real hero who lived in the 1800s. Despite his blindness, Zatoichi could beat any opponent! There are now seventeen Zatoichi movies.

Another unusual group of Japanese films is the baby cart series. In these movies, a Samurai brings his infant son onto the battlefields in a baby carriage. The sight of the baby being wheeled through bloody fight scenes is very weird. The movies have such strange titles as *Baby Cart in Peril* (1972) and *Baby Cart to Hades* (shown here in 1974 as *Lightning Swords of Death*).

Since no one walks around carrying a sword these days, modern Japanese martial arts movies don't use them much—they wouldn't be believable. You do see amazing Japanese forms of martial art such as judo, jujitsu, and karate (karate was brought to Japan from Okinawa in the 1920s). Look for these styles in *The Streetfighter* series starring Sonny Chiba and *Roaring Fire* with Japanese star Hiroyki "Henry" Sanada.

Japanese martial arts movies are not as easy to find in America as the Chinese movies are. They are certainly not shown on TV as often. But as the popularity of martial arts movies grows, we're sure you'll be seeing more and more fabulous movies from Japan.

Ralph Macchio: The Actor Behind the Karate Kid

He's small. He's skinny. But he packs a punch. Audiences loved his determination and spirit in the movie *The Karate Kid*. And now he's back, fighting even more impossible odds in *The Karate Kid II*.

Daniel, the movie's hero, is a good-natured kid who doesn't look for trouble. He's smart, he's funny, and he just wants to have a good time. Unfortunately, life isn't that simple for him. In the original *Karate Kid*, it was the high school bullies who were after him. In the sequel, even more sinister forces menace him and his teacher, Mr. Miyagi.

Ralph Macchio, the actor who plays the lead role, has many things in common with Daniel, and one of them is that both of them are just a bit surprised to wind up as martial artists. As early as age three, Ralph wanted to be a tap dancer. He used to watch old movies with Fred Astaire and

Ginger Rogers and he'd dance along in front of the TV set. Seeing that her son had talent, his mother, Rosalie, enrolled him in a dance school. Ralph was in high school when a talent scout saw him doing an act at his school's dance recital. From there, Ralph began doing TV commercials.

Even though Ralph now takes his acting very seriously, at that early stage of his career he thought the whole thing was just a lark. He once sent a friend to an audition in his place because he didn't want to miss a beach party. (The friend got the part, too!)

Ralph, who was born and raised in Huntington, New York, graduated from high school in 1979. At first, he intended to go to college and study business management. "I wanted to give show business a try," he remembers, "but not bank my life on it because it was a shot in the dark."

That summer, Ralph found out acting was much more than that for him. He was offered a role in the comedy *Up the Academy.* He had to be on location in Kansas for eleven weeks and that's why he didn't enter college right away. And after that first big job, Ralph had changed his mind about his future. He decided to give up business management. He now wanted to study acting seriously.

When Ralph returned home he took a course in public speaking and studied dramatics. He found it difficult at first to overcome his embarrassment at playing serious roles. "In acting class I used to wonder if people would think I looked stupid when I became really emotional, and my teacher said, 'If you're going to think that, go home. You're going to hold back and not give your fullest.' I've learned to drop my guard and let people see what's inside of me." The hard work paid off. Ralph auditioned for and won a part on the TV series *Eight Is Enough*. The show was in its last season and Ralph played the adopted nephew.

Ralph then tried out for a role in the movie *The Outsiders*. It was a serious part and he wanted it badly. "That was the first time in my whole career that I couldn't say I don't care." Ralph got the part of Johnny Cade. Although the movie had a talented cast that included Matt Dillon, it was not a hit. "Somehow it didn't come out right," Ralph admits.

The next movie Ralph made *did* come out right —very right. It was *The Karate Kid*! Actually, Ralph almost didn't get the role. For one thing, he was already 22 but the Karate Kid was supposed to be only 16! But at 5'7" and 130 pounds, Ralph looked young enough to play the part. In this case, Ralph's Italian good looks were working against him, too. The role was originally written for a light-haired boy whose ethnic background would be less clear.

But Ralph's talents got him through the obstacles. And some of his New Yorker's skepticism helped, too. "When I read the title, I thought, is this some kind of joke?" he recalls. He thought it was going to be some sort of Bruce Lee parody. This attitude helped him win the role.

"It was Ralph's cockiness and vulnerability that got him the part," notes director John Avildsen (who also directed *Rocky*). Avildsen had the part rewritten so that the character would be Italian and he hired Ralph.

Turning himself into the Karate Kid was the challenge of a lifetime for Ralph. He had never studied martial arts before, but his dance background and love of soccer gave him a sense of balance and a talent for fast footwork. He embarked on a five-week crash course in karate with martial arts expert Pat Johnson. "I had to do stretches for this that I swear I never thought my body could do," he says.

Ralph admits he's no karate expert, but he did learn enough of the martial art to do his own stunt work. "Only once, when I fall off my bicycle on a hill, did they use a stand-in," he says.

Ralph thinks that karate is just one part of what made *The Karate Kid* such a hit. "It's about a relationship," he says, referring to the father-son type of interaction Daniel has with his teacher, Mr. Miyagi. Ralph thinks that "without that chemistry the movie would have been just a bad version of *Rocky*."

During the filming of the movie, Ralph took a few punches. "The only really unexpected thing that happened," he remembers, "was when Billy Zabka—that's Johnny—was supposed to miss my face with a roundhouse kick, and because our angle was off he hit me hard across the mouth and jaw. When I went down, the cameras kept rolling—they thought I was acting. I wasn't! But the swelling finally went down and we didn't miss any shooting because of it."

Ralph's hard work on *The Karate Kid* paid off. The critics thought he was wonderful—and so did the fans! "I love to sneak into previews to see how audiences react," Ralph says. "I did that with *Karate Kid*—it was great! Sometimes the cheers of the audience were so loud I couldn't hear the dialogue."

For a while, Ralph set his karate image aside and concentrated on other roles. He played a tough teen in the movie *Teachers* and he played a boy who went from age 15 to 90 in a brief time in the TV movie *Billy Grier*.

Ralph then learned to sing the blues for the movie *Crossroads*. For that part, he studied guitar in order to play the part of a guitarist. Ralph agrees that there are similarities between *Crossroads* and *The Karate Kid*. "There's an older guy/father figure in both movies. And the endings are similar, with the audience rooting for the underdog in a battle. In *Karate Kid*, it was the tournament. In *Crossroads*, it's a guitar duel. All in all there are plot similarities in *Karate Kid* and *Crossroads*. And sometimes I worry about it and sometimes I think that it isn't totally bad, because if I take similar situations and play them differently, I'm proving something—I'm a good actor." But Ralph doesn't need to prove he's a good actor anymore. His many fans already know it!

In the two years between the making of *The Karate Kid* and *The Karate Kid II*, it was difficult for Ralph to keep in shape. During the filming of *Billy Grier*, he admits, "I wasn't in good physical shape. I was going out. I was eating garbage. I wasn't exercising." But knowing that *The Karate Kid II* was coming up, he changed all that while he was working on *Crossroads*. "I had a killer schedule. I had to work out during my lunch hours to keep in shape for *Karate Kid II*." He was in for a shock, though, when he found out that without the regular training sessions he could no longer get his kicks above his waist!

Ralph's skills are now better than ever, thanks to his renewed training for *The Karate Kid II*, once again with ninth-degree black belt Pat Johnson. Ralph could never give a real martial artist anything to worry about—but that's not what he wants. He's more interested in making Daniel believable, and that he does incredibly well.

As a person, Ralph is a lot like the parts he plays onscreen. Of course, since he's 24, he's older than most of those characters. "Sometimes it's weird," he says, "because you find yourself much more mature than the characters you play, but it's always interesting. It keeps you young."

When he's not doing a film, Ralph lives with his parents in Huntington. "My folks see me after I get Hollywood's silver platter treatment and they bring me right down to earth," he laughs. Ralph isn't really the movie-star type. "I'm a very clean, very straight person," he observes. "I was just brought up that way. I'm very much a control person—I like to know 24 hours a day what I'm doing."

Some of the things Ralph loves besides acting are playing hockey and listening to Bruce Springsteen. He likes to write, too, especially experimental movie scripts and plays. Ralph doesn't have a lot of time for hobbies, though, since he's one of the busiest young actors around. Will there be a *Karate Kid III*? Maybe so. Ralph committed himself to making *two* more movies after the original *Karate Kid*. So keep your eyes out for *The Karate Kid III*!

THE KARATE KID—HOW REALISTIC IS IT?

The Karate Kid is a terrific movie, but just how true to life is it? Does anyone really learn karate the way Danny did? What goes on in a typical karate school—is it anything like the one where Johnny and the Cobras train? Could Danny, with his two months of training, actually have won a real tournament, fighting against black belts who've trained for years? And what about the other things Mr. Miyagi teaches Danny—the philosophy lessons? Just what do they have to do with the martial arts?

Let's begin with the mysterious Mr. Miyagi, the superintendent in Danny's building. After Mr. Miyagi easily rescues Danny from a group of attackers, he explains that he learned karate in Okinawa from his father.

For anyone interested in the history of karate, Okinawa is a very important place. It is one of the Ryukyu Islands, in the Pacific Ocean off the southern coast of Japan. The islands are also close to the eastern coast of China, so they became "stepping stones" between the two countries. The people of Okinawa absorbed parts of both the Chinese and Japanese cultures. They borrowed the art of kung fu from the Chinese and blended it with their own native fighting systems.

In 1609, a Japanese army of Samurai warriors invaded Okinawa. They conquered the island, took its ruler back to Japan as a hostage, and set up a police force that forbid the Okinawans to carry arms. The Japanese thought that without weapons the islands would be unable to revolt.

But the Samurai hadn't counted on the Okinawan fighting spirit. The islanders immediately began to perfect their martial arts. Many went up into the mountains where the Buddhist monks lived. There they trained by toughening their elbows and knuckles by hitting rough straw pads. They pounded their fists against tree trunks. During this period, the Samurai armor was made of lacquered bamboo and held together by leather thongs. When the Okinawans returned from the mountains with their hardened hands and fingers, they were able to penetrate the Japanese armor easily.

The Japanese decided to stop the Okinawan rebellion by sending in mounted troops. The islanders then created a series of lethal kicks, many of them flying kicks, so that they could take down even a warrior on horseback. They also learned to use common items such as sickles, chains, and sticks as weapons. The Samurai never suspected that a man carrying a sickle used to cut wheat was really carrying a dangerous weapon capable of stopping his own sword.

The Okinawans' brave attempts to drive out the

Japanese were the roots of modern karate. Unfortunately, no matter how hard the Okinawans fought, they were never able to defeat the invaders.

In 1868, more than two hundred years after the Japanese invasion, a man named Gichin Funakoshi was born in Okinawa. He was a poet, an artist, and a master of the island's fighting arts. His fame soon spread, and in 1921 he introduced karate to Japan. Although some experts say the Japanese created their own system of unarmed fighting, most people agree that Okinawa is the birthplace of modern karate. Funakoshi was the man who gave it to the rest of the world.

Now what does all of this have to do with Danny and Mr. Miyagi? Just this: By learning karate from Mr. Miyagi, Danny is learning from one of the most reliable sources possible. In *The Karate Kid II*, Danny journeys even closer to the source of karate when he follows Mr. Miyagi back to Okinawa.

Mr. Miyagi, Danny learns, has some surprising ideas about karate. For instance, he doesn't care about karate belt colors—which usually mark the level of fighting ability of the person who wears it. But when Danny asks Mr. Miyagi what kind of belt he has, the teacher answers, "Canvas belt. It holds my pants up." He doesn't seem to think a black belt is very important. In truth, Mr. Miyagi is no different than the ancient karate masters.

In those early days of karate, there was no system of colored belts at all! The students wore white belts to keep their jackets closed. Gradually, over years of practicing karate, a belt would become grimy with sweat and handling. It would change from white to off-white to brown and finally to black. A black belt was simply a white belt that showed proof of years of training. In his own way, Mr. Miyagi is trying to teach Danny that it's not the outer things—the belts and uniforms —that matter in karate. The martial arts are really about training the fighter inside.

That's why Danny's first lesson is about ideas. On the surface, it has nothing to do with karate. Mr. Miyagi is pruning his bonsai tree and he offers to let Danny help. Bonsai trees are miniature works of art, and Danny knows it. He is very scared to mess with Mr. Miyagi's trees. But Mr. Miyagi tells Danny to close his eyes and form a picture of the tree in his mind. Then he tells Danny to open his eyes and "remember picture, make like picture, trust picture." Still, Danny hesitates. What if his picture is all wrong? "If come from inside you, always right one," answers Mr. Miyagi.

Danny has just done something called meditation. And though he's meditating on a tree instead of karate, the activity isn't all that different from the way Chuck Norris used to prepare for a fight. Before a match, Chuck would picture the fight in his mind and imagine how he would beat his opponent. Even when a fight didn't go exactly as Chuck had imagined it, the meditation helped him concentrate. Chuck was training his mind as well as his body, just like Danny. Today, almost all karate classes begin and end with meditation.

At first Mr. Miyagi refuses to teach Danny karate. "Fighting always last answer to problem," he says. "Karate for defense only." This is, in fact, what every good martial arts school teaches. Fighting is to be used only when there is no other choice.

Trying to prevent more fights, Mr. Miyagi visits the karate school where Johnny and the Cobras train. He plans to tell the karate teacher that his students are beating Danny up. He hopes the teacher will then make the bullies stop. In most karate schools, that's exactly what would happen. Students who abuse karate by using it to hurt others are usually thrown out of their schools.

Like many things in the movie, Johnny's karate school, or dojo, is a blend of fact and fiction. We see the students kneeling to their teacher and practicing drills while chanting, "Show the enemy no mercy!" When two students spar and one falls, the instructor orders the other to "finish him."

Perhaps there are a few martial arts schools run by maniacs where students are taught to win at any cost. But for the most part, martial arts teachers share a philosophy much closer to Mr. Miyagi's. Instead of finishing each other off, students are taught to help each other and to fight with control so that no one gets badly hurt in the dojo.

But there are some things about Johnny's dojo that are typical of most modern-day karate schools. In a traditional dojo, students are expected to bow to their teachers and obey every command. Usually classes consist of kicking, punching, and blocking drills just like the ones the Cobras do. Students practice each move tens, sometimes hundreds of times per class until the movements become natural to do. This is because in a real fight everything happens so fast. There's no time to think, so the body has to respond automatically. Another typical part of a karate class is sparring, when students practice their fighting techniques on each other. Sparring in karate class is more like tournament fighting than street fighting. The emphasis is on control and clean, sharp techniques, not hurting the other guy.

Push-ups, often done on the knuckles, are part of every karate class. They are one of the oldest and simplest techniques for building upper body strength. In addition, knuckle push-ups strengthen the fist and develop calluses on the knuckles. By the time karate students reach black belt level, their hands are often hardened to the point where punching through a board doesn't hurt at all.

Danny and Mr. Miyagi have only two months to prepare for the tournament. In that time, Danny will have to learn enough karate to fight people who've been practicing for years. Mr. Miyagi lays down basic training rules: "I say, you do. No questions." But from there on, the training isn't anything like what Danny's seen at the dojo. In fact, it doesn't seem to have anything to do with karate.

First, Mr. Miyagi tells Danny to wash and wax his large and unusual collection of cars. He gives no hint of how this will help Danny learn karate. His only advice is, "Breathe. Very important." Danny washes and waxes until his arms are sore. Next lesson: sanding a wooden deck, followed by painting a very long fence.

Finally, Mr. Miyagi shows Danny how these chores connect to karate. The washing, waxing, and sanding movements are similar to circular blocks which knock an opponent's kick or punch away from you. The up and down strokes of painting are like wrist and palm-heel blocks which use the base of the palm for protection. Danny has been learning defensive techniques. In the long hours he's spent working on Mr. Miyagi's cars and house, he's actually practiced his blocks thousands of times. The techniques are becoming part of him.

There's another reason why Danny begins his training with chores instead of punches. According to the legends of both kung fu and kendo, the Japanese art of sword-fighting, students had to prove themselves with hard work before the master would teach them.

Traditionally, in China and Japan, when people wanted to study a martial art, they didn't just sign up for classes. Instead they would approach a master of the art and ask permission to study with him. The answer was almost always no. So to prove their sincerity, the rejected students would remain at their master's door through wind, rain, and cold until the teacher agreed to take them in. Once the master admitted them, there was still no kung fu or kendo. Most students found themselves cooking and cleaning house.

Fumio Demura is a sixth-degree black belt in karate and the man who doubled for Pat Morita, who plays Mr. Miyagi, in his fight scenes. He explains that in the martial arts there is something known as *shitei-ai*, which means teacher-student trust. In the past, it began on the day the teacher invited the student in. And it developed as the student worked around the master's house. Finally, the moment arrived when the master trusted the student enough. Then he'd say, "Come inside the dojo, and I'll show you how to do it." According to Demura, Danny's chores not only teach him skills but are a perfect example of *shitei-ai*. By washing, waxing, sanding, and painting, Danny was proving that he was a worthy student, ready to learn the secrets of karate.

If you're wondering why trust was so important to the teachers, remember that originally karate, kung fu, and kendo were not sports. They were deadly methods of fighting. And the masters were very careful to teach these dangerous arts only to those who would not abuse their powers.

Danny's next lessons are more directly related to karate. Standing on the bow of a rowboat, and later a piling on the beach, he works on balance. In his famous book, *The Tao of Jeet Kune Do,* Bruce Lee says, "Balance is the all-important factor in a fighter's stance. Without balance at all times, he can never be effective." The reason is simple: If you're struggling to stay on your feet, you really can't do anything else. Because of this, there are many karate techniques, such as sweeps, where the purpose is to throw an opponent off balance. As far as learning to keep your own balance, very few karate masters give lessons in rowboats or on beach pilings. No, the best martial artists gain this incredible stability through years of practicing stances and kicks.

In his two months of training, Danny doesn't come near the expert black belt level. He's still a beginner—but he's practiced punching, blocking, kicking, and staying on his feet.

Finally, the day of the tournament arrives. It's

time to see just how good Danny is. Will his training be good enough for him to defeat his opponents—people who are seasoned fighters? Only in the movies.

From the time Mr. Miyagi "borrows" a black belt to the moment of Danny's victory, *The Karate Kid* is a little unrealistic. Most tournaments make sure competitors register in advance. This gives officials a chance to check out people who are new to the circuit. Even if a beginner were able to sneak into a full-contact black belt competition, the judges would see at once that he didn't have the skills. They'd stop the fight for safety's sake.

In order to make it to the finals, Danny must fight round after round of black belts. Most of the fighters on the tournament circuit are highly skilled martial artists who've been competing for years. Not only do they like to fight, they're unbelievably good at it. That Danny takes quite a beating is not surprising. That it lasts more than one round is! In spite of the fact that Danny has worked hard and learned courage, in a real tournament he wouldn't have made it past the first punch.

Even if Mr. Miyagi's training methods are a far cry from those of most karate schools, and even if the final fight is more dream than reality, *The Karate Kid* is true to the heart and spirit of the martial arts. "Win, lose...no matter," Mr. Miyagi tells Danny. "Self-respect matter."

84

THE KARATE KID vs. THE KARATE KID II

The Karate Kid and *The Karate Kid II* have very different story lines, but there are a lot of similarities, too. For one thing, Ralph Macchio still plays the lovable Daniel. Mr. Miyagi is once again portrayed to perfection by Noriyuka Pat Morita, using the same combination of gentle good humor and intensity that won him an Academy Award nomination in the original movie. Both films have Daniel and Mr. Miyagi pitted against a threatening situation and using karate to save the day. But that's about as far as the similarities go. The settings of the two movies couldn't be farther apart. While the first movie took place in the familiar world of an American suburb, *The Karate Kid II* brings the audience to the island of Okinawa, karate's birthplace and the childhood home of Mr. Miyagi. In *The Karate Kid*, it was Daniel who needed Miyagi's help. In the second film, Mr. Miyagi is in trouble himself.

Jerry Weintraub, the movie's producer, comments, "Now Daniel is fighting not for competition points in Los Angeles, but is defending himself and his mentor against bitter foes bent on destruction in Okinawa. The danger is not only to Daniel and Miyagi, but to the continued existence of Miyagi's ancestral village and the peaceful way of life it represents. Miyagi seems passive and simple, but underneath he's a warrior and a mystic. Here, we start to understand why."

The supporting cast of characters is also quite different in the second movie. Instead of the average Americans of Daniel's world, we meet the people of Miyagi's homeland. There is the love of Miyagi's youth, Yukia, played by Nobu McCarthy. And there is also a new love for Daniel. The 19-year-old beauty queen, Okinawan-born Tamlyn Tomita, wins Daniel's heart as Yukia's niece, Kumiko.

John G. Avildsen, who is once again the director, comments, "The characters have grown and developed. There's a greater degree of jeopardy involved, with Daniel's life on the line, and the love story between Daniel and Kumiko is more romantic."

The enemy Miyagi and Daniel must face is named Sato. He's a karate master and Miyagi's sworn enemy. Sato's nephew, Chozen, is out to get Daniel as well.

As different as these two movies are, the beautiful relationship between Daniel and Mr. Miyagi remains the same. Director Avildsen notes, "Miyagi represents the father figure most of us wish we had. He has wit and humor." The special feelings between Daniel and Miyagi deepen as Daniel sees another side of his friend. And the fighting in *The Karate Kid II* is even better than in the original. Ralph has improved his karate skills so he can give a really great performance.

Despite the differences in the two movies, the messages of *The Karate Kid* and *The Karate Kid II* are similar at heart—if you stand up for what you believe in, you will find the strength within yourself to triumph despite the odds.

10 FACTS ABOUT
THE KARATE KID
MOVIES

1. The writer of both scripts, Robert Mark Kamen, is a black belt with twenty years of karate training.

2. The movie is based on the real-life story of Michael Dietrich, who was beaten up by local kids shortly after moving to a new neighborhood. After a near-fatal beating, Michael enrolled in karate school and became a black belt. Michael's brother Richard enrolled, too, and became America's youngest black belt at age six.

3. Tamlyn Tomita, who plays Kumiko, was a 1984 Miss Nisei Week Queen and 1985 Miss Nikkei International Beauty Contest winner.

4. *The Karate Kid II* wasn't filmed in Okinawa. It was shot in Hawaii on a millionaire's estate. The city of Naha, Okinawa, was re-created in a Hollywood studio.

5. Noriyuki Pat Morita began his career as a stand-up comedian.

6. Pat Johnson, who trained Ralph Macchio for the part of Danny, also wrote the screenplay for Chuck Norris's *Force of One* and did the action choreography for Norris's *Good Guys Wear Black* and *An Eye for an Eye*. He also worked with Bruce Lee in *Enter the Dragon*.

7. Ralph Macchio says getting his body to look right for the part was extremely difficult. "The diet I was on was a real killer!"

8. Ralph refuses to pose in karate stances because he doesn't want to be thought of as a martial arts star.

9. In the original *Karate Kid*, one of the bad guy Cobras (the one who first hurts Daniel's leg in the tournament) is played by Chad McQueen, son of the late actor Steve McQueen. Chad's father brought him to Chuck Norris's school to learn self-defense after he'd been picked on at school. It was due to Steve McQueen's encouragement that Chuck Norris began seriously to pursue a film career.

10. Pat Morita says of his role: "I like Miyagi. I think he's going to continue for a long time." He based the character on his father's friends.

Vocabulary

Bushido means "the way of the warrior" in Japanese. It is the strict Samurai code of behavior based on honor, loyalty, duty, and obedience.

Dojo is the Japanese word for the "way place," and it refers to the place where the way of the martial arts is practiced—the training hall or martial arts school.

Hung gar is one of the most popular styles of Southern Chinese kung fu, combining Shaolin tiger and crane styles. It is the style most often seen in Hong Kong kung fu movies.

Jeet kune do is a martial arts system designed by the late Bruce Lee. Its philosophy is: be creative and find what works best for you as an individual. Jeet kune do combines many other fighting systems including kung fu, judo, boxing, and fencing.

Jujitsu is an ancient Japanese system of combat, using both armed and unarmed techniques. Jujitsu emphasizes arm locks, throwing techniques, and the use of pressure points.

Judo is the modern, less lethal sport form of jujitsu. Judo uses many wrestling and throwing techniques.

Karate is a Japanese system of unarmed fighting, originally developed on the island of Okinawa. The most common techniques in karate are open-hand strikes, punches, kicks, and blocks.

Kendo means "way of the sword" in Japanese. The system is based on Samurai fighting. Today in the sport of kendo, bamboo swords are used for practice.

Kung fu is a term used to mean a variety of armed and unarmed Chinese fighting systems. Many kung fu styles, such as crane, tiger, and monkey, are based on the ways animals move.

Nunchakas are a weapon made of two or three sticks linked by chains or short ropes. Bruce Lee made these famous in *Enter the Dragon*. They are illegal in most states.

T'ai chi chuan is one of the oldest Chinese martial arts styles. T'ai chi is also known as a soft style because it emphasizes soft movements, the use of breath control, and energy. It is generally not practical for self-defense until the student reaches very advanced levels.

Tae kwon do is a Korean style of unarmed combat similar to karate but it puts more emphasis on kicks.

Tang soo do is another Korean martial arts system that's similar to karate. Tang soo do was developed in 1949.

Wing chun is the only kung fu system developed by a woman, and it is based on the law of economy of movement. This was the style studied by the late Bruce Lee.